D1393472

Catholic Christianity

Getting Started

compiled by
The Catholic Truth Society

*All booklets are published thanks to the
generous support of the members of the
Catholic Truth Society*

CATHOLIC TRUTH SOCIETY
PUBLISHERS TO THE HOLY SEE

Contents

All rights reserved. First published 2013 by The Incorporated Catholic Truth Society, 40-46 Harleyford Road London SE11 5AY Tel: 020 7640 0042 Fax: 020 7640 0046. This edition © 2013 The Incorporated Catholic Truth Society. Second chapter 'A Guide for Christian Living' reproduced with permission of Darton Longman and Todd from The New Jerusalem Bible.

ISBN 978 1 86082 861 4

The Heart of Christianity

Unanswered questions

Many people find it hard to believe in a loving God. They doubt his existence altogether, or their experience of suffering and human tragedy make them doubt his love. Scientists seem to be solving the great puzzles of the universe, and psychologists seek to unlock the deepest mysteries of the human heart.

But there are some questions that don't go away.

- What caused the whole universe to exist in the first place?
- Why is there so much suffering in the world?
- What is the meaning of human life?
- What is the point of my own individual life?
- Is there such a thing as life after death?

These are huge questions. You would be suspicious if someone claimed to answer them with any certainty. There is a limit, surely, to what we can discover for ourselves, and very often we need to admit that some questions are simply beyond human understanding.

God has not left us alone

The heart of Christianity, however, is the belief that God has spoken to us in human history, by sending us his Son. He has not left us alone. He has revealed himself to us. We don't have to go round in circles trying to solve everything ourselves. He has come to our help.

The idea that Christians claim to know the truth about God will sound arrogant or even fundamentalist to many people. But in fact there is a kind of humility behind this claim. It's not that Christians, as people, are special - far from it. It's that they have been given the most extraordinary gift: the knowledge of Jesus Christ. And their desire is simply to share that gift with others. It's Jesus himself who taught that he is the Way to God, and the Truth, and the Life.

The Christian message

What, then, is the Christian message? It is this: that God is love. His love created and sustains the whole universe. His love brings into being every human life. We were meant to live in peace with God and with each other, but this peace was broken through hatred and sin.

In the fullness of time, God sent his only Son, Jesus Christ, to be our Saviour. He came into the world to reveal the love and mercy of God, and to lead us to the Father. Through him we can find peace with God and with each other. His death on the Cross brings us forgiveness. His Resurrection on the third day, and his Ascension to heaven, give us the hope of an astonishing new life. And the gift of the Holy Spirit allows us to share in that life even now on this earth, through faith and through belonging to the Church.

You may not be convinced by these ideas. But at least you can see that the heart of Christianity is not a theory or a programme but a person: Jesus Christ. A person we can come to know, above all through faith.

An invitation to believe

Faith is a gift. We can only believe in Jesus Christ if the Holy Spirit helps us to believe. At the same time, faith is a step that we can choose to take - it is a personal decision. In any human relationship there are moments when we need to trust and to make a commitment - despite our uncertainties. It's the same with God. He calls us to trust him and to reach out to him.

Faith changes everything. It transforms our life, our relationships, our hopes, our love.

Don't be afraid of taking a step in faith. You might do this in different ways. You might speak to a Christian friend about their faith, and find out what it means to them. You might read some of the Bible, or find a Christian book or website that could help you. You might visit a Christian church, and appreciate the beauty and serenity of the building. You might speak to a priest, and put some questions to him, or find out if there is a group for enquirers in a local church that you could join.

An invitation to pray

The simplest and most important way of taking a step in faith is to pray. Don't be afraid to open your heart to God in prayer, however nervous or uncertain you feel. He always responds, even if it is in quiet and unexpected ways. Say to him, out loud if it helps, a simple phrase like: "Lord, help me". "God, have mercy on me". "Jesus, I believe in you". Or simply, "Lord, I want to believe, help my lack of faith". If it is helpful, you could pray with the words of the Lord's Prayer, the Our Father, which Jesus gave us. Or if this is all too much, you could just sit in silence, with the intention in your heart that God would guide you and be with you.

To pray in any of these ways is like opening a door. It allows God to work in your life and reveal himself more and more. Faith is not an irrational leap in the dark, it is a response to the love of God. And perhaps, in the depths of your heart, he is calling you, even if you are not sure how to interpret that call. What matters is that we try to respond. It was Jesus who said, "Ask, and it will be given unto you; search, and you will find; knock, and the door will be opened to you."

The Church

Eventually, if you come closer to Christ in faith, this desire will bring you to the Church. The Church is the community that Jesus himself founded, so that his followers would always have a spiritual home to live in, a family to belong to. This community is found today in its fullness in the Catholic Church.

In the Church we receive the life of Christ in the sacraments; we come to know him through the inspired words of the Bible; we hear his teaching through the bishops and the Pope; and we share in the great tradition of Christian faith that stretches back through the centuries. The Church is a rock that Christ never abandons, despite the sins and weaknesses of her members. It is a spiritual home that will always be a place of safety and security, a place where we can rejoice in the gifts of the Holy Spirit and in the friendship of our fellow Christians.

The love of God

So whatever you feel about your own worth, never doubt that your life has a meaning. God created you for a purpose. He loves you and cares for you. And he is closer to you than you can imagine. You will never find true peace or lasting happiness without him. As St Augustine wrote: "Lord, you have made us for yourself; and our hearts are restless until they rest in you".

Whatever your questions and doubts, don't be afraid to find out more about him and open your heart to him.

A Guide for Christian Living

The heart of Christ's moral and spiritual teaching is given in the Sermon on the Mount (in St Matthew's Gospel, chapters 5 to 7). This is an abridged version. It gives us a vision and guide for Christian living.

The Beatitudes

How blessed are the poor in spirit:
the kingdom of heaven is theirs.

Blessed are the gentle: they shall have the earth as inheritance.

Blessed are those who mourn: they shall be comforted.

Blessed are those who hunger and thirst for uprightness:
they shall have their fill.

Blessed are the merciful: they shall have mercy shown them.

Blessed are the pure in heart: they shall see God.

Blessed are the peacemakers:
they shall be recognised as children of God.

Blessed are those who are persecuted in the cause
of uprightness: the kingdom of heaven is theirs.

Blessed are you when people abuse you and persecute you and speak of all kinds of calumny against you falsely on my account. Rejoice and be glad, for your reward will be great in heaven.

You are light for the world. A city built on a hill-top cannot be hidden. No one lights a lamp to put it under a tub; they put it on the lamp-stand where it shines for everyone in the house. In the same way your light must shine in people's sight, so that, seeing your good works, they may give praise to your Father in heaven.

The Commandments

Do not imagine that I have come to abolish the Law or the Prophets. I have come not to abolish but to complete them.

You have heard how it was said:
You shall not kill. But I say this to you, anyone who is angry with a brother will answer for it. If you are bringing your offering to the altar and there remember that your brother has something against you, leave your offering there before the altar, go and be reconciled with your brother first, and then come back and present your offering.

You have heard how it was said:
You shall not commit adultery. But I say this to you, if a man looks at a woman lustfully, he has already committed adultery with her in his heart. If your right eye should be your downfall, tear it out and throw it away; for it will do you less harm to lose one part of yourself than to have your whole body thrown into hell.

It has also been said:
Anyone who divorces his wife must give her a writ of dismissal. But I say this to you, everyone who divorces his

wife, except for the case of an illicit marriage, makes her an adulteress; and anyone who marries a divorced woman commits adultery.

You have heard how it was said:
You must not break your oath, but must fulfil your oaths to the Lord. But I say this to you, do not swear at all. All you need say is "Yes" if you mean yes, "No" if you mean no.

You have heard how it was said:
Eye for eye and tooth for tooth. But I say this to you; offer no resistance to the wicked. If anyone hits you on the right cheek, offer him the other as well; if someone wishes to go to law with you to get your tunic, let him have your cloak as well. And if anyone requires you to go one mile, go two miles with him. Give to anyone who asks you, and if anyone wants to borrow, do not turn away.

You have heard how it was said:
You will love your neighbour and hate your enemy. But I say this to you, love your enemies and pray for those who persecute you; so that you may be children of your Father in heaven, for he causes his sun to rise on the bad as well as the good, and sends down rain to fall on the upright and the wicked alike. For if you love those who love you, what reward will you get? You must therefore set no bounds to your love, just as your heavenly Father sets none to his.

Humility and prayer

Be careful not to parade your uprightness in public to attract attention; otherwise you will lose all reward from your Father in heaven. When you give alms, your left hand must not know what your right is doing; your almsgiving must be secret, and your Father who sees all that is done in secret will reward you.

When you pray, go to your private room, shut yourself in, and so pray to your Father who is in that secret place, and your Father who sees all that is done in secret will reward you.

In your prayers do not babble as the gentiles do, for they think that by using many words they will make themselves heard. Your Father knows what you need before you ask him.

So you should pray like this:

Our Father in heaven,
may your name be held holy,
your kingdom come,
your will be done,
on earth as in heaven.
Give us today our daily bread.
And forgive us our debts,
as we have forgiven those who are in debt to us.
And do not put us to the test,
but save us from the Evil One.

When you are fasting, put scent on your head and wash your face, so that no one will know you are fasting except your Father who sees all that is done in secret.

Trust in God

Do not store up treasures for yourselves on earth, where moth and woodworm destroy them and thieves can break in and steal. But store up treasures for yourselves in heaven. For wherever your treasure is, there will your heart be too.

No one can be the slave of two masters. You cannot be the slave of God and of money.

That is why I am telling you not to worry about your life and what you are to eat, nor about your body and what you are to wear. Look at the birds in the sky. They do not sow or reap or gather into barns; yet your heavenly Father feeds them. Are you not worth much more than they are? Can any of you, however much you worry, add one single cubit to your span of life?

So do not worry. Set your hearts on his kingdom first, and on God's saving justice, and all these other things will be given you as well. So do not worry about tomorrow; tomorrow will take care of itself. Each day has enough trouble of its own.

Do not judge, and you will not be judged; because the judgements you give are the judgements you will get. Why do you observe the splinter in your brother's eye and never notice the great log in your own? Hypocrite! Take the log out of your own eye first, and then you will see clearly enough to take the splinter out of your brother' s eye.

Ask, and it will be given unto you; search, and you will find; knock, and the door will be opened to you. Everyone who asks receives; everyone who searches finds; everyone who knocks will have the door opened. Is there anyone among you who would hand his son a stone when he asked for bread? If you, then, evil as you are, know how to give your children what is good, how much more will your Father in heaven give good things to those who ask him!

Bearing Good Fruit

So always treat others as you would like them to treat you; that is the Law and the Prophets.

Enter by the narrow gate, since the road that leads to destruction is wide and spacious, and many take it; but it is a narrow gate and a hard road that leads to life, and only a few find it.

Beware of false prophets who come to you disguised as sheep but underneath are ravenous wolves. You will be able to tell them by their fruits. A sound tree produces good fruit but a rotten tree bad fruit.

It is not anyone who says to me, "Lord, Lord," who will enter the kingdom of heaven, but the person who does the will of my Father in heaven. Therefore, everyone who listens to these words of mine and acts on them will be like a sensible man who built his house on rock. Rain came down, floods rose, gales blew and hurled themselves against that house, and it did not fall: it was founded on rock.

What is the Catholic Faith?

It's impossible to summarise the Catholic faith in a few hundred words. This chapter will simply give you an idea of the main areas of Catholic belief, and perhaps encourage you to look into some of them more deeply.

God

There are good reasons for believing in God. Faith is not a superstition or an irrational leap. The existence of the universe points to some kind of creative power that brought it into being and sustains it. The underlying laws of nature cannot have arisen just by chance.

So there is no fundamental conflict between science and religion. Science asks the question:

- How do things work in the world?

Religion asks different questions:

- Why is there any world at all?
- What is my place within it?

The human person

Many animals are remarkably skilled and inventive. But human beings have a distinctive place in creation. Our openness to truth and beauty, our freedom and moral conscience, cannot be explained in purely natural terms. They are spiritual gifts that reflect something of God's own likeness and give us a special dignity.

But human life is fragile and often marked by suffering. We catch glimpses of evil in the world and in our own hearts. We have an intuition that things are not as they were meant to be, and there is a longing in the depths of our hearts for a happiness which is not of this world.

Jesus

God did not leave us alone. He has revealed himself to us. He spoke first to the Jewish people, his chosen ones, through the Law and the prophets. He taught them to wait for the promised Saviour. When the time was right, about two thousand years ago, he fulfilled his promises by sending his own Son to be born of the Virgin Mary in Bethlehem.

Jesus Christ is the Son of God, the only Saviour of the world. He is a human being like us, but without sin. And he is the all-powerful and eternal God, infinite in knowledge and love.

Salvation

Jesus transformed people's lives by his teaching and his miracles. He reached out to them with God's healing and forgiveness. His greatest act of love was to offer his life for us in sacrifice, in obedience to the Father. He let himself experience the depths of human suffering, even to being crucified. His death on the cross brings us forgiveness and reconciliation. It means that nothing has to separate us from the love of God in Christ.

On the third day, God raised Jesus from the dead. Jesus then revealed himself plainly to his followers, and convinced them that he had truly risen from the dead. By ascending to heaven in his glorified humanity he showed that our goal is to be with God for all eternity. After his Ascension, Jesus sent the Holy Spirit to his followers so that they could share in his divine life and proclaim it to others. In this way he revealed the mystery of the Holy Trinity: that within the unity of God there is a communion of Divine Persons - the Father, the Son, and the Holy Spirit - equal in majesty and glory.

Faith

Faith is our wholehearted response to the love of Christ, when we believe in him and entrust our lives to him. Through faith and baptism our sins are forgiven and we are reborn as God's adopted children. We share in God's own life, and the Holy Trinity comes to dwell within our souls.

Faith is a pure gift, given by the Holy Spirit. But faith is also something that we must freely choose, by accepting Jesus as our Saviour and believing in his teaching.

The Church

Faith is never lived alone. Jesus gathered his followers together into a new family called the Church, founded on the twelve apostles. This community would be a sign of his continuing presence in the world, and a place where people could share in the new life Jesus had won for them.

Jesus gave his Church a way of life that is handed on in its Tradition. He gave it the inspired words of the Holy Scriptures, in the Bible. This community that Jesus founded continues today in its fullness in the Catholic Church. The Pope and the Catholic bishops, despite their weaknesses, continue the work of the first apostles as shepherds and teachers of the Church.

The sacraments

Our lives are transformed by the seven sacraments that Christ gave to his Church. A sacrament is a sacred ritual that helps us to see the reality of salvation, and allows that reality to change our lives. The sacraments give us a share in God's own life through the gift of the Holy Spirit and through our response of faith.

Baptism and Confirmation unite us with the death and resurrection of Jesus and make us Christians. Marriage and Ordination give us specific vocations. Reconciliation ('Confession') and Anointing bring us forgiveness and healing. In the Mass, the Holy Eucharist, we share in the once-for-all sacrifice of Christ on Calvary. Through the power of the Holy Spirit, with Christ and with the whole Church, we worship the Father. And in Holy Communion we receive Christ himself as food and drink.

Love

A living faith involves a commitment to follow Christ and to do the Father's will. The heart of Christian morality is the twin commandment to love God and to love our neighbour. It is to love as Christ himself loved.

Christ gives us his own moral teaching in the New Testament, which fulfils the teaching of the Old Testament. He continues to guide us by means of the moral teaching of the Catholic Church in every generation. By living a faithful Christian life we help to build God's Kingdom of peace and justice in this world, and we witness to the power of Christ's love in our lives. If we fail through weakness or sin, we can turn to the inexhaustible mercy of God.

Prayer

In prayer we lift our hearts and minds to God. We praise him and thank him. We ask for his forgiveness and help, for ourselves and for others. All Christian prayer is made 'in the name of Jesus'. This reminds us that we can only reach the Father's heart through Christ, in the power of the Holy Spirit. Christians worship only God, but they also honour the saints and the angels and call on their help - especially the Virgin Mary.

Hope

Death is a frightening mystery that awaits us all. When we die, our spiritual souls will come into the presence of God. We will see the whole truth of our lives. Those who believe in Christ, who freely choose to accept the mercy and salvation he offers, will enter heaven - even though some may need to pass through the purification of purgatory. Those who reject Christ, who freely choose to turn away from the mercy and salvation he offers, will be condemned - condemned by their own actions and choices. For them there will be no possibility of life with God. This is the tragedy of hell.

At the end of time, when Christ comes again, our bodies will share in the Resurrection. God will reveal the hidden purposes of his creation, and reconcile all things in Christ. The just will live in the presence of God for all eternity. The hope of heaven gives us joy even in the sufferings of this life, and gives us reason to keep close to Christ through lives of faith and love.

How to Become a Catholic

Thinking of becoming Catholic?

People from all kinds of backgrounds, and for all kinds of different reasons, express an interest in knowing more about the Catholic faith. You may be engaged, or married, to a Catholic; you may belong to another Christian denomination, perhaps baptised or not, or a member of another religion, or none. You may be searching for the answers to some sincere and important questions about life.

What does the Catholic Church claim to be?

The Roman Catholic Church claims that it is the visible community established by Jesus Christ, and built up by his first disciples, the apostles - we can trace our life back two thousand years to his life on earth and to his teachings and ministry. It is God's will that all men and women should encounter the Christian message, so the Catholic Church is at heart a *missionary organisation*, seeking all the time to encourage people to become Catholics. So, in the first place, Catholics will welcome that you are considering this step in your life by reading this.

How do I get started?

Personal contact is often better than reading a booklet, so the first thing you should do is speak to a priest at a Catholic church near where you live or work. He will be able to talk to you about what is involved in becoming a Catholic; he can talk with you about your life and background, and what it is that has prompted you to make this enquiry.

How do I find out some basic information?

If you don't know where the nearest church is, you'll find that Catholic churches are usually listed in telephone directories. If you can find a church near where you live or work, the best way to be introduced to the Church's life is to go to Mass on a Sunday or a weekday and look at parish newsletters or magazines so you can see something of local Catholic life; there should also be copies of Catholic newspapers which tell you of the life of the Church in the rest of the country and the world.

How does the learning process begin...and end?

Sometimes the priest will offer to help you consider becoming a Catholic by individual sessions with him, so that you can learn about what the Catholic Church teaches and discern God's will for you. This is an important time and it doesn't pay to rush, no matter how enthusiastic you may feel. Alternatively, instruction may be given in groups, with other people in the same position as yourself, which might be called by various names - RCIA (which stands for the *Rite of Christian Initiation of Adults*), Journey of Faith, or something similar. These groups meet over a period of months. Usually adults who wish to become Catholics do so at Easter, during the late night Mass on the Saturday evening before Easter, the Easter Vigil - the greatest feast in the Catholic calendar!

What other things will I need to do to be baptised?

If you have never been baptised, that is 'christened', then if you proceed you will be baptised as an adult and confirmed. If you have been baptised in another Christian church whose rite of baptism the Catholic Church recognises as valid the Catholic community accepts that baptism, and welcomes your experience of Christianity in that church. You cannot be baptised again, so you are confirmed and 'received into full communion' with the Catholic Church, often with others who have to be baptised as adults. In some parishes those who need to be baptised are prepared separately from those who have already been baptised in another church; in others everybody is prepared together.

Catholics, normally as children and as they grow up, receive several sacraments:

Baptism (becoming members of God's Church); the **Eucharist** (receiving Our Lord as the Bread of Life); **Reconciliation**, also known as **Confession** (receiving the forgiveness of sins); and **Confirmation** (receiving the strength to be soldiers for Christ). Depending on your present situation (baptised or un-baptised etc), you may be introduced to all of these along this new journey.

Is there anyone else who can help me through all this?

Usually the whole church community in the parish is invited to support you and an individual layperson will help you as a godparent or sponsor during your preparation period. Usually those who are being prepared are supported in special ceremonies in the months leading up to their becoming Catholics in the local church and the cathedral: this emphasises that when you become a Catholic you are not simply taking an individual step in your life - you are also becoming part of the wider family of the Catholic Church in the local area and throughout the world.

What if I'm not sure about something…or everything?

In these settings, either individually with a priest or in a group, you will have the chance to ask questions about what you are being taught, to share any doubts or problems you may have, and to talk about your own life history and the influences in your life. People will also be able to suggest things you can read: you should certainly get hold of a good modern Catholic edition of the Bible, such as the *New Jerusalem Bible*, and *The Catechism of the Catholic Church*, which explains all the main Catholic beliefs in a comprehensive way.

How else can I help myself?

In addition to this, you might find it helpful to talk to other people you know who are Catholics; they might be friends, members of your family, or people you work with. Being a Catholic isn't always easy, and like the Gospel itself, is challenging: so ask them to be honest with you! God encounters us in many different ways in our lives, and personal contact with other people is a good way of learning about something.

What are the consequences?

As a Catholic you become part of a worldwide community of believers, and of a local parish; you will want to familiarise yourself with Catholic moral and social teaching; you will be responsible as a parent for educating your children in the Catholic faith. Above all as you grow in faith, you will be a true 'light of Christ'.

And what about the future?

The journey doesn't end with Confirmation. As Catholics we should pray every day, take part in the Mass every Sunday and Holy Day of Obligation, live the seasons and feasts of the Church's life, receive the sacraments and live a life of Christian charity towards our fellow man. Christ invited us to deny ourselves, take up our cross and follow him. You are special and unique in the sight of God. He wants the best for you and is leading you to himself. As you reflect on how to become a Catholic, try to be open to God's will.

Signs and Symbols Inside a Catholic Church

Why signs and images?

A Catholic Church, whether old or new, will always be a building rich in signs and symbolism, and likely to contain objects and images not readily understandable to all visitors. However, we know that through our senses we engage with the world and grow in knowledge and so we depend on sight, hearing, touch, smell and taste. The Catholic Church makes use of all five senses to help us grow in knowledge of God and our faith, by way of 'sacramentals' - these are symbols and images designed to help us in our relationship with God, and not simply 'decoration'.

The Sanctuary

The sanctuary is the most important area in the church, within which the priest celebrates the Mass and leads the services. It will usually be raised up a little, or in some other way separated from the rest of the building, while clearly still a part of it.

The Tabernacle

This is the most important object in the building - the living heart of a Catholic Church. The tabernacle is a shrine, usually made of precious metal and often veiled with a coloured cloth. It most often stands in the sanctuary, or perhaps in a small chapel of its own, set aside for private prayer. The tabernacle contains the Blessed Sacrament, the bread consecrated by the priest at Mass which is transformed into the Body of Christ. It is reserved in the tabernacle so that Holy Communion can be taken to the sick, but also so that people can pray in the presence of Jesus, who we believe remains there, body, blood, soul and divinity, under the appearance of bread. Near the tabernacle you will always see a lamp burning - symbolising the living presence of Jesus in the Blessed Sacrament.

The Altar

The altar will always be the most prominent object within the sanctuary, the holy table on which the sacrifice of the Mass is offered. Traditionally, an altar which has been *consecrated* (specially blessed by the bishop) is made of stone and contains relics of the saints - a practice which goes back to the earliest centuries of Christianity. Because the body and blood of Christ will rest here during Mass, the altar is treated with particular reverence: it is covered with a white cloth, and candles are placed on or near it. The priest will kiss it at the beginning and end of Mass, and it may be honoured with incense.

The Ambo or Lectern

Often placed within or close to the sanctuary, from here the Word of God (scripture) is proclaimed during the Mass and other liturgies. If the altar is the 'first table', the ambo is a 'second table', of the word. Homilies, sermons and prayers are often given from the ambo, which is usually made of wood or stone, and can be elegantly decorated or covered, and treated with reverence.

The Font

The font is the place where infants (and occasionally adults) receive baptism. It can be located in a separate part of the church (called a baptistery), or may be found in or near the sanctuary.

Paschal Candle

Often near the font, this very large decorated candle is placed on a high stand: a new paschal candle is blessed each year at the Easter Vigil, and is lit throughout the Easter season and afterwards for every baptism and funeral - a powerful symbol of Jesus Christ, Light of the World and our hope of eternal life.

Aumbry

Near the font there may also be an aumbry, a special cupboard containing the holy oils used for baptisms, confirmations and anointing the sick.

Holy Water

This is another reminder of baptism which is found in stoups, or bowls, near the doors of a Catholic Church - on entering we make the sign of the cross with the holy water, which has been blessed by the priest, and can also be taken away for use in people's private devotion at home.

Crucifix or Cross

Another important image in the church is the crucifix which hangs somewhere near the altar: the image of Jesus on the cross reminds us of his supreme, loving sacrifice which is represented for us at every celebration of the Mass.

The Sacred Heart

A familiar image of Jesus which will be found in almost every Catholic Church is the Sacred Heart, showing Jesus displaying his wounded heart - another reminder of his wonderful love. Devotion to the heart of Jesus is very old, but is especially associated with St Margaret Mary Alacoque, who lived in the seventeenth century.

Stations of the Cross

These fourteen pictures, or carvings, which can be elaborate or very simple, depict the final journey of Jesus to Calvary, from his judgement by Pilate to his burial in the tomb. Usually set on the walls, Catholics use this set of images in their private prayers or sometimes - especially during Lent - at a public service.

Images of the Mother of Jesus

Catholics venerate Mary as Mother of God, and in a special way as the spiritual mother of all Christians. In honouring Mary we honour her Son, and we believe that she will always pray for his disciples. Catholics worship God alone, but we *honour* Mary as a person uniquely close to Jesus Christ. Thus we can be sure of finding in any Catholic church a statue, or at least a picture, of the Blessed Virgin Mary (Our Lady) often depicted holding the infant Jesus.

Images of the Saints

Usually churches will contain images of certain other saints. Catholics believe that the thousands of Catholic saints are our friends, and seeing their image inspires us to be like them. The choice for a particular church will depend on its history, location and dedication, and other special circumstances. A saint very often depicted is St Joseph, the foster-father of Jesus: either holding the Christ Child, or sometimes with a carpenter's tools. Others are St Anthony, St Patrick, St Jude and St Thérèse of Lisieux.

Vestments and Colours

During Mass the priest wears special vestments. These derive from the clothing commonly worn by people during the first centuries of Christianity. Secular fashion changed, but the Church kept to the old style. Thus it was that clothing once common to all, became the distinctive dress of the clergy. The colour of these vestments, and very often the veil of the tabernacle and other hangings will vary according to the season of the Church's year.

- **Purple**, a colour of penance and expectation, is worn during Advent and Lent. It is also appropriately worn at funerals, when we pray for the deceased on their final journey to God.

- **White**, a joyful colour, is worn at Christmas and Easter, and for feasts of Our Lady and many saints.

- **Red**, colour of fire and blood, is worn on feasts of the Holy Spirit and in commemorating the suffering of Jesus and his martyrs.

- **Green**, symbolic of life and growth, is worn on the Sundays in Ordinary Time.

- **Rose-coloured** vestments may be worn to mark the middle Sundays of Advent and Lent.

- **Black**, the colour of mourning, remains an option at funerals and for All Souls' Day (2nd November), though not so common now.

- **Gold and silver** vestments may be worn on very important feasts, such as Easter and Christmas.

The Liturgy

At Mass, there will be a further use of symbols: the use of **candles, incense and bodily gestures** (kneeling, bowing, genuflecting etc) involve all the senses in our act of worship and reverence.

If you are becoming a Catholic, or discovering these things for the first time, they can seem confusing. Time taken to learn about them will help you to appreciate them more as an appropriate response to the unfathomable riches of our Christian faith.

How to Pray

"Teach us to pray"

Jesus' disciples said to him: "Lord, teach us to pray" (*Luke* 11:1). Today, too, many people find themselves asking the same thing. The Catholic Church has a wonderful tradition of prayer on which to draw. Unfortunately, many Catholics still see prayer as something complicated and difficult, or reserved for 'professionals' (perhaps priests and religious sisters). This is the first myth to slay! Prayer is not complicated and it is meant for everyone. An early Christian poet, St Ephraem, wrote: "Birds fly, fish swim, people pray." Human beings are made to pray, because they are made for God.

Contemplative prayer

All prayer is valuable, even the most short and spontaneous, but the prayer that goes deepest, and truly touches the heart, is the form of prayer known as contemplative, or mental prayer. Again, the terminology can put people off: but it shouldn't. All prayer can be defined very simply - 'conversation with God'. In contemplative prayer the conversation is longer than usual, and to help prevent our minds wandering, we make use of a few basic rules. But the rules are very simple, and mental prayer can be made by anyone. As St Teresa of Avila said "Contemplative prayer is nothing else than a close sharing between friends; it means taking time frequently to be alone with him who we know loves us."

One form of prayer

Over the centuries, the Church and its saints have developed many different forms of mental prayer. The one outlined here is a simple one, a form made popular by St Francis de Sales in the 17th century, and used by millions of people ever since. St Francis aimed especially at the laity and people living in the secular world: he believed all were called to holiness, and all to prayer.

Finding a place to pray

Prayer is not complicated, but it needs patience and dedication. Finding appropriate surroundings is important: the great saints can pray anywhere and any time, but most of us are not so fortunate! Try and find a quiet place where you won't be disturbed. If you have access to a church, that would be ideal - or the opportunity to pray before the Blessed Sacrament, even better. But a quiet room in your house will work just as well. It is also important to pray in an appropriate posture: sitting upright or kneeling, helps to keep most people alert and attentive.

Giving time to prayer

How long should you pray for? As long as you can! It is obviously better to pray for five or ten minutes than not at all. That said, we do need to be generous with God, and practical - giving time to prayer allows us to listen as well as speak. Many people find it useful to give a set amount of time each day to prayer - 'beginners' might like to start with, say, ten minutes. This may increase as time goes by. In time, some find half an hour or even an hour a day is what they grow to like and need. Set yourself a realistic target - and stick to it. Don't be tempted to cut short your prayer because you may find it difficult at first - treat it as important, and persevere.

When to pray

What time of day is best for prayer? Well, we can pray at any time, morning, afternoon or evening. Realistically though, most people are more alert in the mornings. The later we leave our prayer, the more tired and distracted we may become.

The presence of God

When you come to pray, wherever it is, first remind yourself that God is there. Then consciously place yourself in his presence, and ask him to help you.

Lifting your mind

To come to prayer, we need to focus our minds on God. There are many ways to do this. You might read a brief passage from the Gospels, look at an icon or a crucifix, reflect on one of the Mysteries of the Rosary (the Rosary, incidentally, is itself an excellent form of mental prayer, if prayed reflectively). You can close your eyes. Be still and try to enter into your own heart, and quietly repeat a simple phrase, sincerely, such as "Lord Jesus, have mercy on me, help me". Don't be in a hurry. Once God has filled your thoughts - talk to him. Tell him you believe in him, hope in him, love him. Tell him your troubles and say sorry for your sins. This is prayer.

Distractions

Unless we are very focussed or very holy, our minds soon get distracted. From thinking of God, we soon find ourselves thinking of food, work, and our families. Don't be distracted by distractions. Even the saints suffered from them, and they are not important. If you find your thoughts have wandered, simply bring them back again (read another verse of the gospel - fix your gaze on the icon - repeat your phrase). Distractions never entirely disappear, but they will grow less with practice. Don't be discouraged by them. They are quite normal. To pray can in this sense involve a bit of a battle.

Listening

In this way - thinking of, talking to, and loving God - our time of prayer will soon pass. But it is important that we listen too - a listening of the heart. If we treat God as a real friend - if we tell him our troubles, our difficulties and our temptations - then in prayer, he will show us the answers to all these questions, helping us to see things in a new perspective, with fresh understanding. Even the most insoluble problems can be resolved in prayer.

Conclusion

When our time of prayer is almost finished, there are three final things we should do.

1. Try and find something to 'take away' with you - perhaps a word of scripture, an idea or an image - something to remind you of your prayer throughout the day.

2. If appropriate, make a resolution: resolve to act as God has guided you in your prayer (and if you still feel a lack of guidance, ask God to show you the way forward).

3. Give thanks to God for this time of prayer, and ask him to remain with you always. You may want to end by saying a brief prayer of your own choice, such as the Our Father.

It is hard to write about prayer, because it is something that needs to be experienced. If you really want to learn to pray, then the only way to do it is to try. Set aside the time. Open your heart, and persevere - you will never look back, and you will never regret it.

Everyday Catholic Prayers

Sign of the Cross

In the Name of the Father, ✠ and of the Son,
and of the Holy Spirit. Amen.

Our Father

Our Father, who art in heaven,
hallowed be thy name;
thy kingdom come,
thy will be done
on earth, as it is in heaven.
Give us this day our daily bread,
and forgive us our trespasses,
as we forgive those who trespass against us;
and lead us not into temptation,
but deliver us from evil.
Amen.

Glory be

Glory be to the Father,
and to the Son,
and to the Holy Spirit.
As it was in the beginning, is now, and ever shall be,
world without end.
Amen.

Apostles' Creed

I believe in God,
the Father almighty,
Creator of heaven and earth,
and in Jesus Christ, his only Son, our Lord,
who was conceived by the Holy Spirit,
born of the Virgin Mary,
suffered under Pontius Pilate,
was crucified, died and was buried;
he descended into hell;
on the third day he rose again from the dead;
he ascended into heaven,
and is seated at the right hand of God the Father almighty;
from there he will come again to judge the living and the dead.

I believe in the Holy Spirit,
the holy catholic Church,
the communion of saints,
the forgiveness of sins,
the resurrection of the body,
and life everlasting. Amen.

Act of contrition

O my God, because you are so good,
I am very sorry that I have sinned against you,
but by the help of your grace, I will not sin again.

Act of faith

O my God, I believe in you and all that your Church teaches because you have said it and your Word is true.

Act of hope

O my God, I hope in you for grace and for mercy
because of your promises, your mercy and your power.

Act of charity

O my God, because you are so good,
I love you with my whole heart
and for our sake, I love my neighbour as myself.

Prayer to the Holy Spirit

Come, Holy Spirit, fill the hearts of your faithful,
and enkindle in them the fire of your love.

V. Send forth your Spirit and they shall be created
R. And you shall renew the face of the earth.

Let us pray.

O God, who taught the hearts of the faithful
by the light of the Holy Spirit,
grant that by the gift of the same Spirit we may always be
truly wise and ever rejoice in his consolation.
Through Christ our Lord. Amen.

Grace before meals

Bless us ✠ O Lord, and these thy gifts,
which we are about to receive from thy bounty,
through Christ our Lord. Amen.

Grace after meals

We give you thanks, almighty God,
for these and all your benefits,
who livest and reignest, world without end. Amen.
May the souls of the faithful departed, ✠ through the
mercy of God, rest in peace. Amen.

Morning offering

O Jesus, through the most pure Heart of Mary,
I offer you all the prayers, the works, the sufferings
and the joys of this day
for all the intentions of your Divine Heart
in the Holy Mass.

At the Stations of the Cross

I love you Jesus, my love above all things.
I repent with my whole heart of having offended you.
Never permit me to separate myself from you again.
Grant that I may love you always, then do with me what
you will.

Prayer for the dead

Eternal rest, grant unto them O Lord,
and let perpetual light shine upon them.
May ✚ they rest in peace. Amen.

Commendation

Jesus, Mary and Joseph,
I give you my heart and my soul.
Jesus, Mary and Joseph,
assist me in my last agony.
Jesus, Mary and Joseph,
may I breathe forth my soul in peace with you. Amen.

For a happy death

Into your hands, O Lord, I commend my spirit.
Lord Jesus, receive my soul.

Prayer to the Sacred Heart

O Sacred Heart of Jesus I implore
the grace to love you daily more and more.
(said three times)

In honour of the Blessed Sacrament

O Sacrament most holy, O Sacrament Divine,
all praise and all thanksgiving be every moment thine.

The Divine Praises

Blessed be God.
Blessed be his holy Name.
Blessed be Jesus Christ, true God and true man.
Blessed be the name of Jesus.
Blessed be his most Sacred Heart.
Blessed be Jesus in the most holy Sacrament of the Altar.
Blessed be the Holy Spirit, the Paraclete.
Blessed be the great Mother of God, Mary most holy.
Blessed be her holy and Immaculate Conception.
Blessed be her glorious Assumption.
Blessed be the name of Mary, Virgin and Mother.
Blessed be Saint Joseph, her most chaste spouse.
Blessed be God in his Angels and in his Saints.

To the Blessed Virgin Mary, Angels and Saints

Hail Mary

Hail Mary, full of grace, the Lord is with thee.
Blessed art thou among women,
and blessed is the fruit of thy womb, Jesus.
Holy Mary, Mother of God,
pray for us sinners,
now, and at the hour of our death. Amen.

Salve Regina

Hail, holy Queen, mother of mercy,
hail our life, our sweetness and our hope.
To you do we cry, poor banished children of Eve.
To you do we send up our sighs,
mourning and weeping in this vale of tears.
Turn then, most gracious advocate,
your eyes of mercy towards us
and after this, our exile, show unto us
the blessed fruit of your womb, Jesus.
O clement, O loving, O sweet Virgin Mary.

V. Pray for us, O holy Mother of God.
R. That we may be made worthy of the promises of Christ.

The Memorare

Remember, O most loving Virgin Mary,
that it is a thing unheard of
that anyone who had recourse to your protection,
implored your help, or sought your intercession,
was left forsaken.
Filled therefore with confidence in your goodness,
I fly to you, O Mother, Virgin of virgins.
To you I come;
before you I stand a sorrowful sinner.
Despise not my words, O Mother of the Word of God,
but graciously hear and grant my prayer.

The Angelus

(said at 6am, 12 noon and 6pm)

V. The Angel of the Lord declared unto Mary.

R. And she conceived by the Holy Spirit.
   Hail Mary, full of grace…

V. Behold the handmaid of the Lord.

R. Be it done unto me according to your word.
   Hail Mary, full of grace…

V. *(with head bowed)* And the Word was made flesh.

R. And dwelt among us.
   Hail Mary, full of grace…

V. Pray for us, O holy Mother of God.

R. That we may be made worthy of the promises of Christ.

Let us pray.

Pour forth, we beseech you, O Lord,
your grace into our hearts,
that we, to whom the Incarnation of Christ, your Son,
was made known by the message of an angel,
may by his passion and cross,
be brought to the glory of his resurrection.
Through the same Christ our Lord. Amen.

The Regina Caeli

(In Eastertide, instead of the Angelus, at 6am, 12 noon and 6pm)

V. O Queen of heaven, rejoice! Alleluia.

R. For he whom you were worthy to bear, Alleluia.

V. Has risen as he said, Alleluia.

R. Pray for us to our God, Alleluia.

V. Rejoice and be glad, O Virgin Mary, Alleluia.

R. For the Lord has risen indeed, Alleluia.

God our Father, you give joy to the world by the resurrection of your Son, our Lord Jesus Christ. Through the prayers of his mother, the Virgin Mary, bring us to the happiness of eternal life. Through Christ our Lord. Amen.

Prayer to St Michael

Holy Michael the Archangel, defend us in the day of battle. Be our safeguard against the wickedness and snares of the devil. May God rebuke him, we humbly pray, and do thou, O Prince of the heavenly host, by the power of God, thrust down to hell Satan and all the wicked spirits who wander through the world for the ruin of souls. Amen.

Prayer to your Guardian Angel

O Angel of God, my guardian dear, to whom God's love commits me here, ever this day/night be at my side, to light and guard, to rule and guide. Amen.

A form of morning prayers

- Sign of the Cross
- Morning Offering
- Our Father
- Hail Mary
- Apostles' Creed
- Glory be
- Come Holy Spirit
- Act of Faith
- Act of Hope
- Act of Charity
- Prayer to the Sacred Heart
- Prayer to your Guardian Angel

Conclude by saying:

May the Lord bless us, ✠ keep us from all evil, and bring us to everlasting life. Amen.

A form of night prayers

- Sign of the Cross

Now make an Examination of Conscience. Afterwards, say:

- Act of Contrition
- Our Father
- Hail Mary
- Apostles' Creed
- Commendation
- Prayer for the Dead

- Prayer to your Guardian Angel
- Glory be
- Prayer to St Michael
- Prayer for a Happy Death

Conclude by saying:
May the Lord bless us, ✝ keep us from all evil, and bring us to everlasting life. Amen.

Further Reading

Reasons to Believe by Adrian Lickorish (EX45)

Christianity: An introduction to the Catholic Faith by David Albert Jones (DO859)

What Catholics Believe by Fr John Redford (DO531)

Compendium of the Catechism of the Catholic Church (DO742)

Companion to Prayer (DO652)

Companion to Faith by Nick Donnelly (DO860)

A Simple Prayer Book (D665)

The Blessed Sacrament (LF12)

Why go to Mass? by Bishop Michael Evans (DO639)

25 Tough Questions on the Catholic Faith ed. by Mgr Keith Barltrop (DO798)

Useful websites:

- CTS Website: *www.CTSBooks.org*
- Catholic Answers: *www.catholic.org*
- Integrated Catholic Life: *www.integratedcatholiclife.org*
- Eternal Word Television Network: *www.ewtn.com*